Stewart, Judy
  Moroccan family, —(Beans)
  1. Morocco—Social life and customs
  —Juvenile literature
  I. Title   II. Series
  964'.05   DT312
  ISBN0-7136-2641-0

A & C Black (Publishers) Limited
35 Bedford Row, London WC1R 4JH

© 1985 A & C Black (Publishers) Limited

Acknowledgements
The map is by Tony Garrett

All rights reserved. No part of this publication may be reproduced, stored in a retrieval system, or transmitted in any form or by any means, electronic mechanical, photocopying, recording or otherwise, without prior the permission of A & C Black (Publishers) Limited.

ISBN 0-7136-2641-0

Filmset by August Filmsetting, Haydock, St Helens.
Printed in Hong Kong by Dai Nippon Printing Co. Ltd.

Moroccan Family

Judy Stewart
Photographs by Jenny Matthews

A & C Black · London

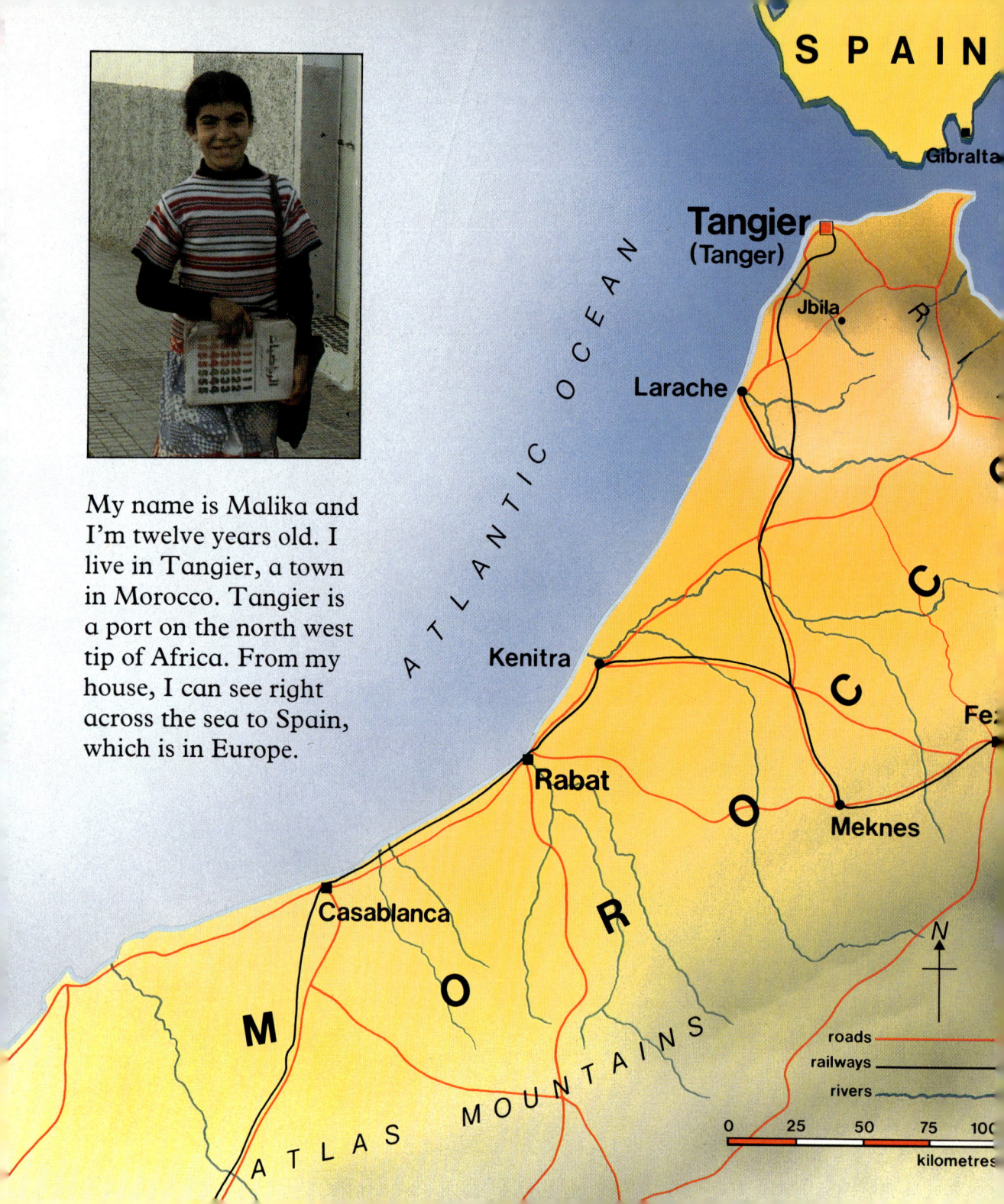

My name is Malika and I'm twelve years old. I live in Tangier, a town in Morocco. Tangier is a port on the north west tip of Africa. From my house, I can see right across the sea to Spain, which is in Europe.

MEDITERRANEAN SEA

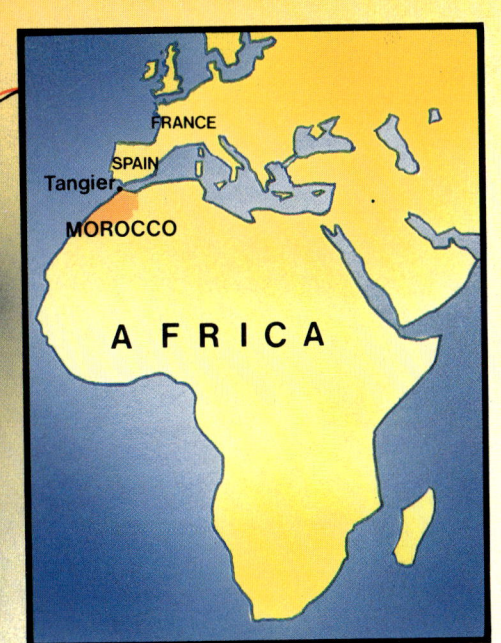

FRANCE
SPAIN
Tangier
MOROCCO

AFRICA

I've got two brothers and four sisters. My sister Fatima is the oldest, she's sixteen. The others are all younger than me. Here they are, walking along the seafront with me and my mum. My brothers are called Mustafa and Karim, and my little sisters are Naima and Rashida. My youngest sister, Aisha, is being carried on Mum's back.

Mum's wearing a jellaba, which is a long coat with a big hood. She's wearing a veil over her face, too. In Moroccan towns, married ladies often cover their faces when they go out, because of modesty. But you can see when Mum's laughing behind her veil.

This is our house. It has a kitchen and a storeroom downstairs and two rooms upstairs.

Mum and I are downstairs in the kitchen, making bread. We eat bread with all our meals and use pieces of bread to scoop up our food. Mum makes four big round loaves of bread every day.

It's hard work making bread. First you must knead the dough and leave it to rise, then you knead it again. I get really puffed when I try, so Mum usually has to finish it.

When Mum's cooking or doing the housework she often carries Aisha on her back. Aisha never cries when she's carried like that. It keeps her out of mischief as well!

Before school, I put the bread on a wooden board, called a 'wasala', and carry it to the baker's oven in the next street. On the way, I meet my friends taking their bread to be baked. We race each other, trying not to drop the bread. The loaves never get mixed up in the baker's oven, because every family stamps a special mark on them.

Mum buys most of our food at the market. She goes there nearly every day. In Tangier, the market is a very noisy crowded place. Cars honk their horns and men shout 'Balek! Balek!', 'Mind out!' as they push loaded carts through the crowds of people doing their shopping.

The shops and stalls sell almost everything you can think of. There are rows of butchers' shops next to rows of vegetable stalls, spice stalls and many others. They all have their different smells and colours.

On Thursdays and Sundays, people from the nearby villages come to sell eggs and vegetables, and to buy what they need from the town. The women wear big straw hats and bright striped skirts. Mum prefers to buy from them because she knows the food is fresh.

I like the orange stalls best. In winter and spring, we eat oranges almost every day. We also put sweet-smelling orange-flowers in our tea, and orange-flower water in our cakes and puddings.

Morocco is famous for its oranges. If you drive south from Tangier, you can see huge groves of orange trees. Lorry–loads of oranges are brought to Tangier and then sent by ship to Europe.

My family speaks Arabic, like most people in Tangier. Some people from other parts of Morocco speak a language called Berber. Our grocer speaks Berber, but he can speak Arabic, too.

At school, we learn to read and write Arabic. You read Arabic from right to left. Here is my name in Arabic. Mum says that Malika means 'Queen'.

ملكة بكالي Malika Bakkali

I go to the same school as Naima and Mustafa. It's just down the road, so we can easily walk there. We have our lessons at different times. There aren't enough classrooms in the school for everyone to have lessons at the same time. Luckily, this means that there is always someone at home to help Mum.

We have lessons in arithmetic, the history and geography of Morocco, French and religious studies, as well as Arabic. History is my favourite subject.

Our teacher told us that Morocco was once a much bigger country. It stretched all the way to Northern Spain. That's why so many places in Spain have Arabic names. Later, the French and Spanish came to rule Morocco.

A lot of people in Tangier still speak French or Spanish, although Morocco became an independent country before I was born. I've been learning French for two years, but I'm not very good at it.

Morocco is a Muslim country and in religious studies we read the Koran. This is the Muslim holy book. We often learn parts of the Koran for homework. The garden is our favourite place for learning, because we can read out loud without disturbing anybody.

After school, if there's nothing else to do, I can watch TV for a while. Because we're so near to Spain and Gibraltar, we get their TV programmes as well as ours. I don't understand Spanish or English, so I only watch the cartoons. They really make me laugh!

Mustafa spends most of his time after school playing football with his friends. He only stops if there's a football match on TV.

Once a week I go to the 'hamam', or Turkish bath, with my sister Fatima. This 'hamam' has three rooms, each one hotter and steamier than the last.

In the hottest room, there are taps where you can get hot water for washing. The water is heated by a wood-burning stove outside the baths. We spend ages sitting in the hot steamy rooms, soaping and shampooing and eating oranges. I scrub Fatima's back and she scrubs mine. You end up very clean, but when you come out you must be careful not to get cold.

Friday is a special day for Muslims so there's no school on that day. This means that our family can have lunch together at mid-day. We usually have 'cous cous' on Fridays. 'Cous cous' is made from flour rolled into tiny balls and steamed in a special pot. It's served with meat and vegetable stew on top.

The old way of eating 'cous cous' was to make a ball of it in the palm of your hand, roll it on to your thumb and pop it into your mouth. But this takes a lot of practice, so we use spoons.

We all eat from a big dish in the middle of a low round table. Before the meal, a kettle of water and some soap is passed round and everybody washes their hands. (We do this after the meal too.) Then we all say 'Bismillah', which means 'in the name of God', and we can begin.

On Fridays, Dad goes to pray at the mosque round the corner. He leaves his shoes by the door of the mosque, just like we do when we go into the house. Mum usually prays at home.

Muslims are supposed to pray five times a day. We know when it's time to pray because a man calls from the top of each mosque to remind us. Then people stop whatever they're doing, get out their prayer mats and face Mecca. This is a town in Saudi Arabia. It's a holy place for Muslims.

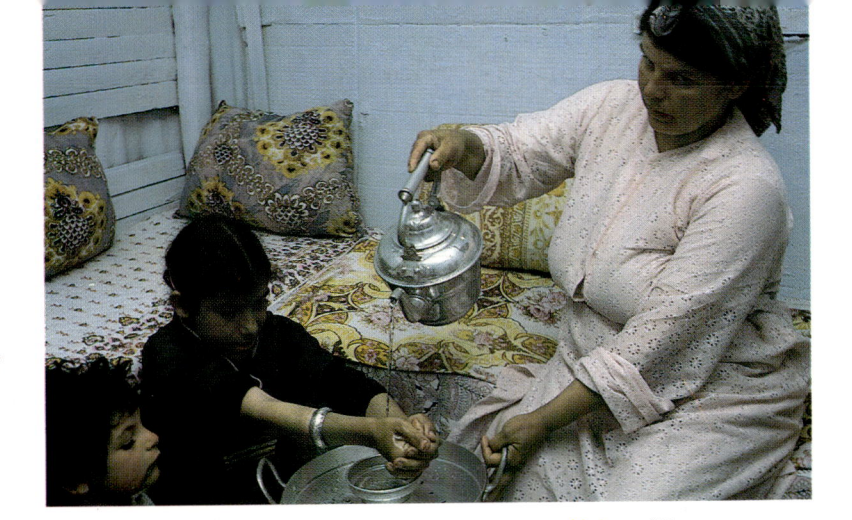

Dad works as a weaver. His workshop is in a narrow street in the old part of town. It's close to a lot of other weavers.

Here's Dad weaving some cloth on his loom. He has two looms which he made himself. Dad can weave six metres of material a day. He sells it for about 50 dirhams a metre. In Tangier, a chicken costs 20 dirhams and a litre of Coca cola (my favourite drink) costs about 2 dirhams.

Sometimes Dad goes to the countryside to buy wool which is spun by the village women. Before he threads the wool on the loom, he winds it on to a wooden frame to stop it from getting tangled.

Dad makes lots of beautiful things from wool. But nowadays, more and more people prefer to buy material made in textile factories. There are lots of these factories in Tangier and other big towns. The material from the factories isn't made of real wool and it doesn't last as long. But it's cheaper and more fashionable.

When Dad doesn't have much work to do, he goes to his favourite cafe to drink tea, chat to his friends or just watch people pass by. The man sitting next to him is wearing a jellaba made of Dad's material. He's got his hood up to protect him from the sun. A jellaba hood can be used as a shopping bag, too!

Dad has lived in Tangier all his life, but Mum was born in a mountain village called Jbila. It's eighty kilometres from Tangier. We sometimes go there to visit my uncle Mohamed and my aunt Zakia.

To reach my uncle's village, we take the bus early in the morning and then we have a long walk. There are no roads to Jbila. We have to cross a stream and then walk up the hill for an hour.

On the way, we meet people going down the track from the village. Some are on mules or donkeys and some on foot like us. They say hello and ask us for news of Tangier. We've brought lots of presents. There's tea, sugar and oil, as well as sweets for the children.

Uncle's house is the first one in the village. There are only fifteen houses in Jbila and there are no shops, cafes or schools. But, like all villages in Morocco, Jbila has a special place where children learn to read the Koran.

Uncle built his house with some help from the neighbours. It's made of home-made bricks baked in the sun, and the walls are whitewashed with lime. Next to the house, there's a garden where the family grows vegetables.

Uncle also has one hectare of land down in the valley. My cousin Abdullah is ploughing the land so that it will be ready for planting. He's going to grow wheat and barley.

I love visiting my uncle. Everyone gets up at dawn and there's always plenty to do. In the morning, Aunty milks the goats and the cow. Then the goats are sent out to join the village flocks. Uncle Mohamed has fifteen goats, as well as a cow and her calf. Their milk is made into cheese, butter and buttermilk. The family also keeps chickens for eggs and meat.

As soon as we wake up, I go with my cousins Hafida and Aziza to fetch water from the spring. It tastes much better than the water at home. In Tangier, we have a water tap in the house. I never realized how much water we used until I came here and had to carry all the water in buckets.

Aunty makes even more bread than we do at home. She grinds wheat into flour on a grindstone in her neighbour's house. Then she makes balls of dough and pats them into round flat loaves.

The loaves are baked in a clay oven behind the house. Aunty gets a fierce fire going inside the oven. Then she puts out the fire and brushes away the ashes. She sprinkles the oven with water before putting in the bread. It doesn't take long for the bread to bake.

Every Tuesday, my cousin Abdullah saddles up the mule and goes to the country market. It's half a day's journey away. Markets are named after the day of the week on which they are held. The nearest market to Jbila is called Souk El Tleta, or 'Tuesday market'.

Abdullah's taking vegetables and chickens to sell. He wants to buy new sandals, oranges and paraffin for the lamps.

If the family needs something special, they usually sell one of their goats. But last year, there was a drought which killed half the animals in the village. Uncle lost a cow and eleven goats.

The family doesn't have much land, so Abdullah is thinking of coming to Tangier. He wants to look for a job so that he can earn more money. Many people leave the countryside to look for work in towns like Tangier or Casablanca. They usually go where they have relations to help them. Abdullah will probably stay with us.

After three days with Uncle, it's time to go home. Aunty gives us lots of vegetables, some freshly baked bread and two chickens for Mum. 'Come again soon', she calls as we set off down the hill in time to catch the bus home.

We get home in the afternoon. Mum has a friend round for tea. We often have visitors in the afternoons. Usually they are aunts or cousins or neighbours. Mum gives them tea and cakes.

Moroccan tea is very sweet, almost like honey. Mum puts a handful of green china tea into the silver teapot. Then she adds boiling water, lots of sugar and a big bunch of mint. The tea is poured into thin glasses. It's polite to drink at least three glasses of tea.

The sugar which Mum uses for tea comes in a 'qaleb', or sugar loaf. Each one weighs two and a half kilos. Rashida's carrying a sugar loaf in from the kitchen. It's almost as big as she is.

Our silver teapot was given to Mum when she married. In Morocco, women are often given a tea-set on their wedding day. Mum's teapot came from a place called Manchester, in England. The best Moroccan teapots used to be made there.

I know a lot about England because Dad's brother, Uncle Salem, lives there. He comes to see us every summer. One day he is going to come back and live in Tangier again. He has already bought some land and is going to build a house.

Lots of tourists come to Tangier for their holidays. They don't speak Arabic but some of them speak French. They come to buy the beautiful things in the bazaars – silver tea-sets and amber jewellery, leather bags and fine wool carpets. Sometimes they peer into Dad's workshop and he offers them a glass of tea.

Tourists also come here for the beach. Tangier has a lovely sandy beach. In summer it's crowded with tourists as well as holidaymakers from other parts of Morocco, where the weather gets too hot. Because of the sea breezes, Tangier hardly ever gets very hot.

This picture was taken in spring when it's a bit too cool to swim. Can you see the animals walking along the beach? They are for the tourists to ride. It's early in the morning and the tourists are all in their hotels having breakfast.

Sometimes I go with my brothers and sisters to play on the beach. I'm too shy to talk to the tourists, but Mustafa sometimes calls 'hello' to them in French or asks the time and we all giggle.

When I'm older, I'd like to go and see the countries where the tourists come from. Maybe I could visit Uncle Salem and be a tourist in England.